THE **SCIENCE** OF **HISTORY**

T009032

SCIENCE ON THE
UNDERGROUND
RAILROAD

by Tammy Enz

CAPSTONE PRESS
a capstone imprint

Published by Capstone Press, an imprint of Capstone
1710 Roe Crest Drive, North Mankato, Minnesota 56003
capstonepub.com

Library of Congress Cataloging-in-Publication Data
Names: Enz, Tammy, author.
Title: Science on the Underground Railroad / Tammy Enz.
Description: North Mankato, Minnesota : Capstone Press, [2023] | Series: The science of history | Includes bibliographical references and index. | Audience: Ages 8–11 | Audience: Grades 4–6 | Summary: "The Underground Railroad was used by people escaping enslavement in the South. This system of passages and safe houses helped people reach freedom in the northern United States or Canada. Did you know science played a role in the Underground Railroad? Learn how people used the night sky to find their way north and much more!"—Provided by publisher.
Identifiers: LCCN 2022008775 (print) | LCCN 2022008776 (ebook) | ISBN 9781666334760 (hardcover) | ISBN 9781666334777 (paperback) | ISBN 9781666334784 (pdf) | ISBN 9781666334807 (kindle edition)
Subjects: LCSH: Underground Railroad—Juvenile literature. | Fugitive slaves—United States—History—19th century—Juvenile literature. | Science—Miscellanea—Juvenile literature.
Classification: LCC E450 .E59 2023 (print) | LCC E450 (ebook) | DDC 973.7/115—dc23/eng/20220310
LC record available at https://lccn.loc.gov/2022008775
LC ebook record available at https://lccn.loc.gov/2022008776

Editorial Credits
Editor: Erika L. Shores; Designer: Heidi Thompson; Media Researchers: Jo Miller and Pam Mitsakos; Production Specialist: Tori Abraham

Image Credits
Alamy: Design Pics Inc, 33, IanDagnall Computing, 34, Randy Duchaine, 45, Science History Images, 43, The Print Collector, 16, Universal Images Group North America LLC, 41; Bridgeman Images: New York Public Library, 36; Getty Images: Dorling Kindersley, 19, duncan1890, 5, 7, ehrlif, 38, ivan-96, 9, Keith Lance, 39, Layne Kennedy, 15; Shutterstock: Everett Collection, Cover (bottom), 8, 11, 18, 31, 35, grandbrothers, 26, gritsalak karalak, 24, Ingrid Maasik, 23, ivector, 17, KamimiArt (design element), KF2017, 28, Mara Fribus, 13, Max Zvonarev, 22, Morphart Creation, 21, 37, 44, Natallia Zhdanouskaya, Cover (top), 1, Sofin Aleksandr, 14, solar22, 27; The New York Public Library/Schomburg Center for Research in Black Culture, Photographs and Prints Division, 25

All internet sites appearing in back matter were available and accurate when this book was sent to press.

TABLE OF CONTENTS

Words in **bold** text are included in the glossary.

CHAPTER 1

AN ENSLAVED LIFE

Enslavement is a system where one person is legally allowed to own another person. This evil system was part of early U.S. history. As early as the 1600s, many African people were brought by force to what is now the United States. They were made to work without pay in homes and fields. Most of these enslaved people lived in the southern part of the United States.

Fact

About 40,000 to 100,000 enslaved people used the Underground Railroad to find freedom.

By the early to mid-1800s, most of the northern states had **abolished** enslavement. But nearly four million enslaved people continued to live in the South. Many sought their freedom. With the help of free Black people, white **abolitionists**, and a secret network called the Underground Railroad, many escaped. This secret network started sometime in the late 1700s. It ran until after the Civil War (1861–1865) when enslaved people finally gained their freedom. They were not considered U.S. citizens until 1868, with the addition of the Fourteenth Amendment to the U.S. Constitution.

Picking crops was one of the many backbreaking jobs enslaved people were forced to do.

The Underground Railroad was not an actual railroad. But the people and places on the path to freedom used code names from the railroad system. The "passengers" were the enslaved people seeking freedom. The "conductors" were the people helping them move to freedom. The "stations" were the safe places where the freedom seekers stayed.

It's likely the Underground Railroad got its name because the railroad was a new technology at that time. Steam-powered trains were just beginning to connect cities across the nation. The trains heated coal to make steam. Steam is water heated to at least 212 degrees Fahrenheit (100 degrees Celsius) that turns into a gas. The gas pushes through the system, moving **pistons** back and forth. The pistons connected to the wheels, making them turn.

The Underground Railroad didn't use actual trains. But science and technology played a big role in the Underground Railroad too.

Steam-powered trains started to become widely used in the 1830s.

Science can help us understand how enslaved people were able to escape. But certain technological developments of the time also explain why enslavement continued in the American South. Enslavement grew there because there was a lot of farmland. Landowners needed workers to help produce crops like tobacco, rice, and cotton.

Fact

The cotton gin could process 50 pounds (23 kilograms) of cotton in a day. By the mid-1800s, the United States was producing 80 percent of the world's cotton.

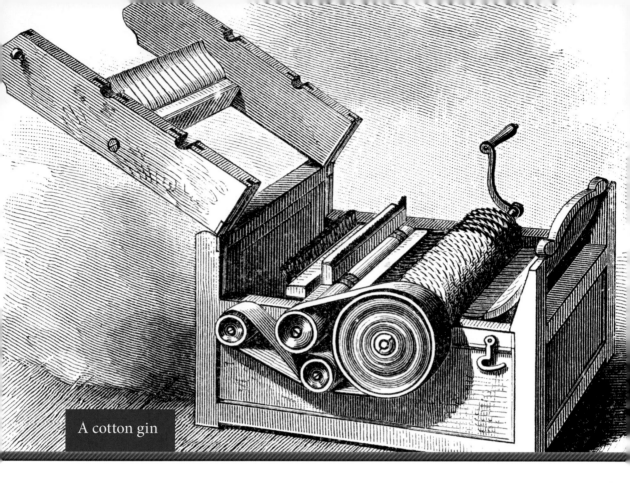

A cotton gin

Cotton became an important crop in the South. Eli Whitney invented the cotton gin in 1793. Before Whitney's machine, cotton seeds had to be removed by hand. It took a long time to process cotton, so it wasn't profitable to produce. The gin combed through cotton fibers and screened out the seeds. Now cotton could be made into cloth quickly and easily. But then more workers were needed to plant and harvest more cotton. Instead of hiring and paying workers, landowners chose to continue their devastating system of enslavement.

CHAPTER 2

MAKING A BREAK FOR FREEDOM

People fleeing enslavement were brave and resourceful. They had to be creative to survive their escape. Hidden dangers and trackers lurked everywhere. If captured, punishment was harsh and sometimes deadly.

Some freedom seekers went south to Mexico. But most headed to the free northern states or Canada. Enslaved people rarely had maps. Most traveled at night. They used the stars to find their way.

The earth spins on an imaginary line that runs through the North and South poles. As the earth spins, stars appear to move in the sky. But one star stays in the same place. This is because it is directly above the North Pole. This star is called the North Star or Polaris. Enslaved people knew to find the North Star. They traveled toward it at night.

People escaping enslavement arrive on the banks of a river in Pennsylvania, a free state.

To find the North Star, enslaved people first looked for a cluster of stars called the Big Dipper. The Big Dipper looks like a cup with a long handle. It appears in different places in the sky during different seasons. In spring and summer, it is high in the sky. In fall and winter, it is much lower.

The two bright stars on the front edge of the cup are called pointer stars. Imagine a line going straight upward through the North Star. If you measure the distance between the pointer stars and multiply it by five, you'll find the North Star. No matter where the Big Dipper is in the sky, this method always works to find the North Star.

Fact

For thousands of years people have used objects in the sky to find their way. Astronomy is the science of all things outside of Earth, including stars, planets, and comets.

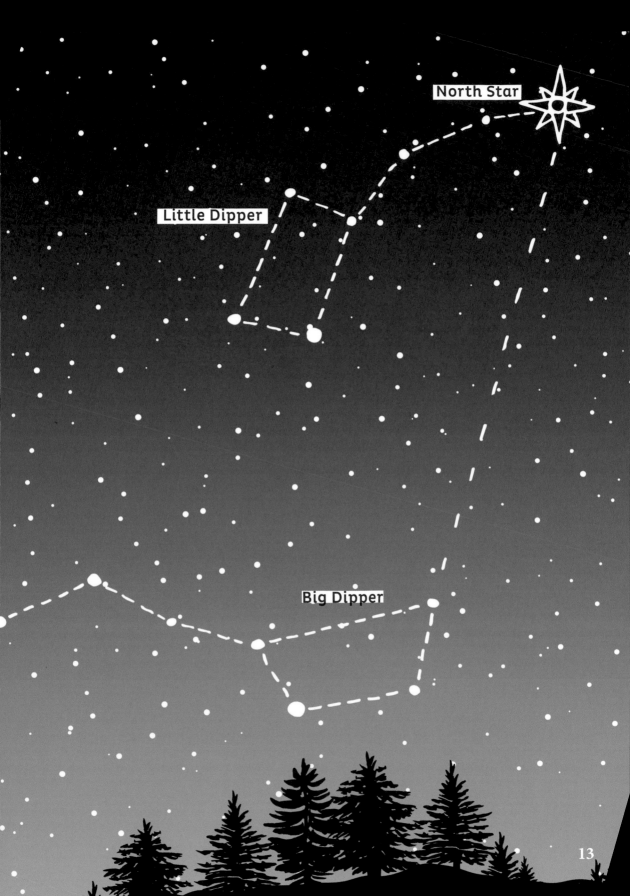

North Star

Little Dipper

Big Dipper

13

Because the Underground Railroad operated in secret, people used signals and code words. Code words had secret meanings. Only people working with the Underground Railroad understood them. For instance, "heaven" meant freedom and "River Jordan" meant the Ohio River. A lamp placed in a certain window would send a message to passengers that it was safe to approach a station. To other passersby the lamp would have no meaning.

An oil-burning lamp

In the 1800s, homes didn't have electric lighting. They had oil-burning lamps. These lamps used wicks. The wick is a piece of cotton put into a cork and placed in a bowl of oil. The oil slowly moves up the wick. When it is lit, the oil burns to give off light.

John Rankin was a minister and a conductor on the Underground Railroad. His house on the Ohio River had 100 stairs leading from the river. Passengers on the Railroad looked for the lamp in the house window to know it was safe to climb the stairs and enter. Inside the house were secret rooms to keep them safe.

John Rankin's house still stands on the Ohio River in Ripley, Ohio.

Once people escaping enslavement were discovered missing, enslavers or their hired trackers set out to capture them. These trackers searched for the smallest detail or sound to find which way a freedom seeker went. They often brought dogs called bloodhounds. They could follow a freedom seeker's scent. Footprints were a big giveaway. So were broken branches or bent stems of grass. To avoid leaving signs, freedom seekers often walked in streams to hide their scent and their footprints.

A freedom seeker runs through a swamp with a dog in pursuit.

People escaping enslavement also listened carefully to hear if they were being followed. Sounds are **vibrations** that travel on waves. The waves bounce off objects to carry sound along. Sound waves weaken as they move. They travel faster through **denser** materials. For instance, sound travels faster in water than in air because water is denser than air. By listening carefully, the people escaping could guess how far away the trackers were.

Long sound wave lengths make low-pitched sounds. Short wave lengths make high-pitched sounds. Humans hear waves vibrating between about 20 and 20,000 vibrations per second.

0 Hz   16 Hz   20 000 Hz

sound too low to hear

sound people can hear

sound too high to hear

People escaping enslavement needed to travel 10 to 20 miles (16 to 32 kilometers) per night. They had hundreds of miles to cover. Science helps explain how they could travel in the darkness of night.

Our eyes need light to form an image on the back part of the eye called the retina. The pupil is the opening at the front of the eye that changes size to let in the right amount of light to see an image clearly. In bright light the pupil becomes very small to only let in a little light. At night it opens to capture as much light as possible.

Freedom seekers had to travel at night in all kinds of weather.

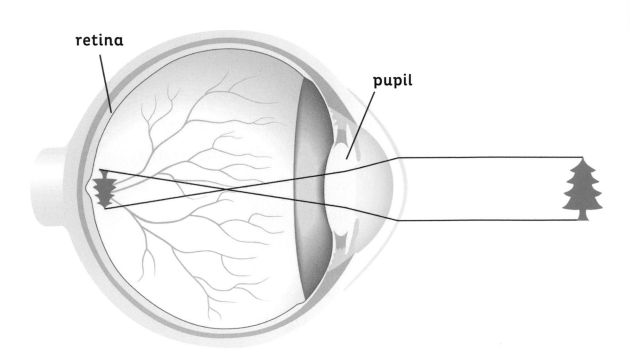

The longer we stay in the dark, the better our night vision becomes. After about 10 minutes in the dark, a chemical activates in the eye. It increases night vision. After an hour or two our eyes improve even more. So, after traveling for a few hours, passengers on the Railroad would have good night vision. They would see better than an enslaver who had just stepped into the dark to look for them.

Science also helps explain how cotton clothing helped people escaping enslavement. The cloth that many enslaved people produced also helped in the trek to freedom. Cotton was a main cash crop in the American South. It grew well in the weather and soil conditions of the area. It also has physical properties that make it helpful in the hot, humid weather.

Cotton clothing has been used as far back as ancient India. While people who were escaping enslavement had very few pieces of clothing, most of what they did have was made of cotton. Cotton is a natural-wicking fiber. It pulls sweat away from your skin to make you feel cooler and dryer. It can hold up to one-fifth of its weight in water before feeling wet. But cotton fibers are also insulating. Cotton clothes helped people stay cool and dry in the humid weather. It helped them stay warm in winter too.

Fact

Cotton is the most-used clothing fiber in the world. Seventy-five percent of the world's clothing contains at least some cotton.

Carrying food that wouldn't spoil was important. Spoiled food can cause food poisoning. The main cause of food spoilage is bacteria. Bacteria are **microorganisms** that live everywhere. They break down cells in food. Bacteria grow with warmth and moisture. Removing water keeps food safe.

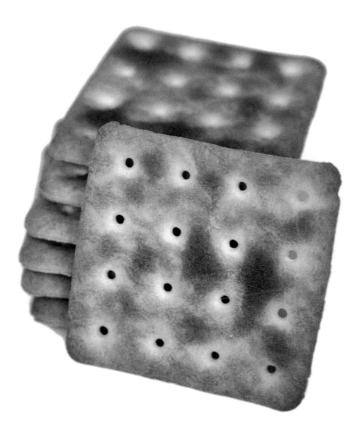

Biscuits called hardtack did not spoil easily like other food.

Soaking pieces of fish in salt kept the food from spoiling.

Hardtack was a staple food for soldiers, travelers, and freedom seekers in the 1800s. These biscuits of flour, water, and salt were baked until they were hard and dry. They weren't very tasty. But they could last for a long time because they had no moisture.

If passengers on the Railroad were given meat, it also had to be preserved. People did this using salt. Salt draws water out of cells to remove moisture. Drying meat by rubbing it with salt or soaking it in saltwater kept it from spoiling.

Some freedom seekers traveled in full view during the day on trains or in wagons. With the help of abolitionists, they pretended to be servants on an errand. Some, especially those with lighter-colored skin, sometimes dressed in fine clothes as **camouflage**. They pretended to be white citizens traveling the country.

But many made the trek to freedom on foot. If enslaved people were given any shoes at all, they were often ill-fitting and cheap. Many went barefoot. Although this was painful, science can help explain how walking barefoot helped them escape. When skin experiences friction through rubbing or pressure, a person's **immune system** kicks in. It tries to fight back. At first, skin develops painful blisters. But if the pressure and friction continue, the skin will form a layer of dead skin cells. These are called calluses. They make feet tougher.

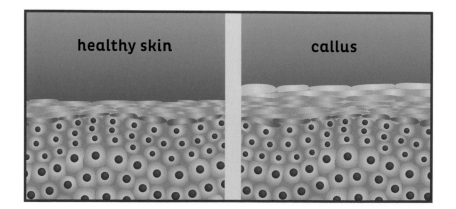

Trackers clomped through marshes and woodlands in heavy boots. But the people escaping enslavement could move quietly through the woods on their bare feet.

Walking barefoot was brutal, but it did allow freedom seekers to keep their footsteps quiet.

CHAPTER 3

DANGERS ON THE TRIP

People escaping enslavement traveled through wet areas filled with mosquitoes. Malaria is a disease that spreads through mosquito bites. Science helps us understand why most people escaping enslavement did not die from this disease.

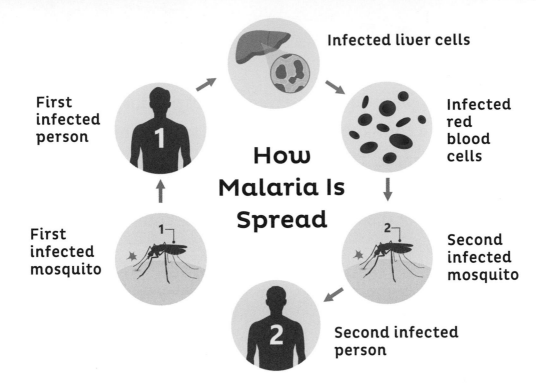

How Malaria Is Spread

First infected person

Infected liver cells

Infected red blood cells

First infected mosquito

Second infected mosquito

Second infected person

Malaria thrives in warm, humid climates like the American South. The disease didn't originally exist in the Americas. It was brought there by colonizers. Malaria also existed in Sub-Saharan Africa. That area was the homeland of many people forcibly brought to America and enslaved.

The disease was very deadly to **Indigenous** people and Europeans. Their immune systems had not been exposed to it before. But many Africans had built up a resistance over time. Their immune systems had gradually developed to fight malaria.

For people escaping enslavement, fearing for their lives was a constant. They always had to be on high alert for danger. That included water moccasins. These deadly snakes are also called cottonmouths. The inside of their mouths are white like cotton.

A cottonmouth

The cottonmouth lives in swamps and wetlands in the American South. People escaping enslavement needed to cross these swamps, often at night. Accidentally disturbing or stepping on a cottonmouth could be deadly.

The venom in a cottonmouth's bite contains **hemotoxins**. They break down blood cells. These toxins keep blood from clotting. A bite from a cottonmouth sends venom through a person's body. It causes internal bleeding. The venom also damages muscle and tissue.

Fact

Today, scientists have developed an antivenom that can reverse the effects of a cottonmouth bite. But in the 1800s, a bite would likely be deadly.

Thirst and **dehydration** were always a risk for a freedom seeker. Water is necessary for life. People need to drink water every day to survive. About 60 percent of our bodies are made of water. It is in every cell. Water helps form cells, control body temperature, and release waste.

But passengers on the Underground Railroad could never be sure the water they found was safe to drink. Often, water contains animal waste or other toxins. Even water that appears clear can have bacteria and viruses that are too small to be seen. These microscopic organisms can attack human cells and cause sickness or death.

Treating water with a chemical called iodine or boiling it can kill these organisms. Doing this makes water safe. Both iodine and boiling kill harmful bacteria. But treating water on the run was often risky and time consuming. People escaping enslavement often had to drink what was available.

Freedom seekers camp near a body of water.

Fact

Adults need about 13 cups (3 liters)
of water each day.

CHAPTER 4

THE FREEDOM TRAIN

There were strict punishments for people who helped freedom seekers. So stationmasters found creative places to hide people. People escaping enslavement needed places to rest until nightfall, before moving to the next stop. Barns, churches, caves, and houses were used to hide the passengers. Often, hidden rooms in walls or under floors were used.

Fact

The Fugitive Slave Act of 1850 placed a $1,000 fine on anyone helping an escapee. That amount today would be about $36,000.

House walls and floors look solid. But they are not. If you pull away the smooth flat boards on walls or floors, you see that they are supported by other thicker boards spaced a little ways apart. These are called studs in walls and joists in floors. A person could squeeze between these studs or joists to move into a hidden room or cellar. When the smooth boards were replaced, no one could see the hidden space. Escapees could hide out until they found a safe way to travel to the next spot on the Railroad.

A secret staircase lies below open boards in a floor.

Travel methods on the Underground Railroad varied. Some enslaved people walked. Others were hidden in trains and wagons. Some people may have used tunnels during their escape. Because there were so many ways to travel and hide, freedom seekers were hard to find. It was impossible to stop the flow of people going north.

Some wagons were fitted with false floors. These floors were built a little higher than the wagon floor. Between the two floors was a gap big enough to hide a person. The wagon looked just like any other wagon from the outside.

Wagons could be made with secret hiding places to carry people north.

If tunnels were used, they may have stretched between homes or sheds. Tunnels also may have connected caves to house basements. Tunnels through loose soil needed brick or wood supports to help the soil arch around the opening.

Henry Brown's Escape

Henry "Box" Brown chose a creative way to get north. He packed himself in a shipping box and mailed himself from his home in Virginia to the home of abolitionists in Philadelphia. The box traveled by wagon train and boat and took 27 hours. When the box was opened, Brown popped out singing.

Enslaved people seeking freedom almost always had to cross a river on their journeys. The conductors would often find a boat or raft to carry a freedom seeker across a river at night. Night crossings were the safest. During the day people hid among packages and crates.

Underground Railroad conductors meet their passengers after they make a river crossing.

A simple raft of logs could be made to help carry freedom seekers across rivers.

Sometimes enslaved people had to make a dangerous crossing on their own. Wading or swimming across a river only worked if it was shallow or narrow. Crossing a deep or wide river required a freedom seeker to find something buoyant to float across the river on. Things are buoyant if they float and are less dense than water. Boats, with air-filled compartments, are less dense than water. Their downward force is less than the upward force of water. That's why they float.

Even a raft made of heavy logs is buoyant because the tiny cells in the wood are air-filled. That makes them less dense than water. The lower density makes the raft float.

If a person felt sick during their escape, it was unlikely that they could see a doctor. The passengers on the Underground Railroad would have used whatever treatments were available. Very little was known about how sickness and disease spread at that time. Few people knew that bacteria and viruses caused sickness. Now we know that tiny microorganisms invading the body cause illness. Medicines are targeted at the virus or bacteria.

A medicine bag filled with herbs and tonics

In the 1800s, herbs and tonics were used to treat sick people. A popular medicine used by conductors on the Railroad was paregoric. It was given for stomach upset, cough, pain, and to calm crying babies. Paregoric contained alcohol and the powerful drug opium.

CHAPTER 5

LIFE IN FREEDOM

People escaping from enslavement still had to be careful after reaching the North. Sometimes trackers found them. They forced them back into enslavement. But many freedom seekers found a new life in the North. And many became conductors on the Railroad. They used their networks to support the Union in the Civil War.

One of the key factors that led to the Civil War was the efforts to abolish enslavement across the nation. The Confederate Army of the South fought to keep a lifestyle based on enslavement. The Union Army of the North fought to end it.

Spying on the opposing army was a key strategy to learn their plans and weaknesses. The Underground Railroad worked in secret. They communicated through codes and hidden signals. They used their network and knowledge to spy on the Confederate Army. They sent information back to the Union Army.

Fact

Besides the Underground Railroad, new spy technology was used in the Civil War. The Union Army used hot-air balloons. Balloonists floated over the countryside to gather information about the location of armies.

In 1863, President Abraham Lincoln issued the Emancipation Proclamation. It said all enslaved people were free in the South. Yet enslavement would continue in many places until 1865.

Advances in the steam printing press helped spread Lincoln's proclamation throughout the country. Metal letters were set on two spinning drums with paper running between them to print on both sides. Heated water called steam pushed the drums to spin. The spinning drums printed hundreds of copies of the news. The steam printing press could print thousands of pages in an hour.

Even though the news was out, it would take until the Thirteenth Amendment in 1865 to end slavery in all states. Now previously enslaved people could move more freely. It was the end of the Underground Railroad.

Workers operate a steam printing press.

When the war ended, science and technology expanded. The railroad system spread across the nation. The electric generator and the internal combustion engine were invented. They led to the development of many new devices such as automobiles and indoor lighting.

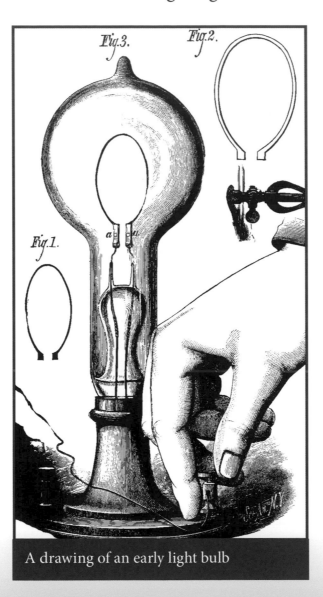

A drawing of an early light bulb

The internal combustion engine uses a spark to ignite pockets of fuel inside it. The energy released from the burning fuel causes movement of mechanical parts. This engine was key to the advancement of the automobile.

The new technology created job opportunities for the newly freed people. The creativity and courage of people involved in the Underground Railroad served them well as they faced new challenges in the free nation.

Fact

Lewis Latimer was the son of escaped enslaved people. He helped Thomas Edison design his famous light bulb.

GLOSSARY

abolish (uh-BOL-ish)—to put an end to something officially

abolitionist (ab-uh-LI-shuhn-ist)—a person who worked to stop enslavement

camouflage (KA-muh-flahzh)—coloring or covering that makes animals, people, and objects look like their surroundings

dehydration (dee-hy-DRAY-shuhn)—the loss of water or body fluids

dense (DENS)—having its parts packed together

hemotoxin (HEE-muh-tok-sin)—poison that breaks down blood cells

immune system (i-MYOON SISS-tuhm)—the part of the body that protects it from germs and disease

Indigenous (in-DI-juh-nus)—a way to describe the first people who lived in a certain area

microorganism (mye-kro-OR-gan-iz-um)—a life form that can't be seen without a microscope

piston (PIS-tuhn)—a machine part that moves up and down within a tube

vibration (vye-BRAY-shuhn)—a back and forth movement

READ MORE

Petry, Ann. *Harriet Tubman: Conductor on the Underground Railroad*. New York: Amistad, 2018.

Smith, Nikki Shannon. *Ann Fights for Freedom: An Underground Railroad Survival Story*. North Mankato, MN: Stone Arch Books, 2019.

Yomtov, Nel. *The Emancipation Proclamation: Asking Tough Questions*. North Mankato, MN: Capstone, 2021.

INTERNET SITES

Discover the Transatlantic Slave Trade to the 13th Amendment
artsandculture.google.com/story/AQURlUKgLy7KaA

Steam Engines
explainthatstuff.com/steamengines.html

The Underground Railroad
kids.nationalgeographic.com/history/article/the-underground-railroad

INDEX

ABOUT THE AUTHOR

Tammy Enz holds a bachelor's degree in Civil Engineering and a master's degree in Journalism and Mass Communications. She teaches at the University of Wisconsin-Platteville and has written dozens of books on science and engineering topics for young people.